A Handbook for

AIR RAID WARDENS

Prepared by Training Section

OFFICE OF CIVILIAN DEFENSE

Revised Edition

U. S. Government Printing Office, December 1941, Washington, D. C.

This Book Belongs to:

---   ------------------------
    (First name)   (Initial)   (Last name)

My Home Address Is:

My Telephone Number Is:

I am _____ *Warden of*

Post No. _____, *City of* _____

State of _____

In case of emergency, notify:

PREFACE

This is one of a series of civilian defense handbooks prepared by the United States Office of Civilian Defense. The purpose of each handbook is to instruct the individual enrolled civilian defense worker in his duties, and to serve as a manual for reference.

The measures for safeguarding civilians against the effects of air attack, which are described in the following pages, have become a necessary part of the defensive organization of any country open to air attack.

Every State and municipality should take such legal or administrative action as may be necessary to provide for the organization, direction, and training of its Air Raid Warden Service.

F. H. LaGuardia,
U. S. Director Civilian Defense.

Washington, D. C.
August 25, 1941.

CONTENTS

	Page
Preface	III
Chain of Command for Wardens	1
The Air Raid Warden's Post	3
Number of Wardens	3
Equipment of Air Raid Warden's Post	5
Post Equipment	5
Warden's Equipment	6
Office Lay-out	6
Your Duties as Air Raid Warden	7
Duties Preliminary to Air Attack	7
Detailed Knowledge of the Sector	8
Signs and Guides	11
The Air Raid Warden in War	12
Use of the Warden's Whistle	13
If No Bombs Fall	14
When Bombs Fall	14
Where and How To Report	16
Keeping the Log	19
Fire Watchers	19
Warden Addresses	21
Handicapped People—Deaf and Blind	22
"If I were a Warden"	22
Coordination of Services	24
Notes	26
Blackouts	29
Warning System	32
What To Do In An Air Raid (Home)	34
Magnesium Bomb, controlling	36
Fire Extinguishers	39
War Gases	41
Gas-tight Room	42
Decontamination	43
Citizens' Defense Corps	45
Manual of Drill	47

A Handbook for

AIR RAID WARDENS

Chain of Command for Wardens.

In a local plan of Civilian Defense, the Air Raid Warden Service may be set up under the Chief of Police or as an independent group. In either case, there will be a Chief Air Raid Warden and the number of administrative links will depend upon the size of the city or cities under the Local Defense Organization.

The basic unit of Civilian Defense is a *Sector* containing the homes of about 500 people. This is controlled by a Warden's Post, staffed by a Senior Warden and three or more Assistant Wardens.

In general, from 4 to 15 Posts are grouped under a Precinct Warden. In smaller cities, they will report directly to the Chief Warden; in larger cities it will be desirable to group Precincts under Zone Wardens.

Fill out names and addresses in the form on the following page.

ADMINISTRATIVE OFFICERS, AIR RAID WARDEN SERVICE

This post No. _____ City _____

　Senior Warden _____

　Address _____

　Telephone _____ Alternate phone _____

This post reports to precinct No. _____

　Zone or Precinct Warden _____

　Address _____

　Telephone _____ Alternate phone _____

Chief Warden of city _____

　Address _____

　Telephone _____

　Note.—The above form is for administrative use and does not represent the communication system for use during air raids. See pages 16–18.

The Air Raid Warden's Post.

The basic unit of Civilian Defense against air attack is a Sector containing the homes of about 500 people. Its extent will depend on the character of the homes. One apartment house may easily accommodate 500 people. Where detached houses are the rule, a number of blocks or squares may form a Sector.

On the following page, draw a map of your Sector, putting in the names of all the streets, marking the limits of your Sector with a heavy line.

In each Sector is a Warden's Post. This may be a single room or suite of rooms or a fitted-up cellar. It must be large enough to serve as a point of assembly for all Wardens of the Sector together with messengers and any other personnel assigned. As a message center, it should afford protection from bomb blast and splinters and should be sealed against war gas. In congested districts, Air Raid Wardens' Posts may be grouped in larger quarters, provided no Warden must travel more than five to eight blocks or squares from that point to cover his district.

The Warden's Post must be plainly marked for the public and small signs should be placed at various points within the Sector to show how to reach it. Luminescent signs made with special paint or fluorescent signs activated by black light are visible during a blackout to persons nearby. Such signs are desirable.

Mark on the map the location of your Air Raid Warden's Post.

Number of Wardens.

Each Air Raid Warden's Post must have from three to six Wardens. The exact number depends

Theoretical Warden Sector
with Standard Symbols

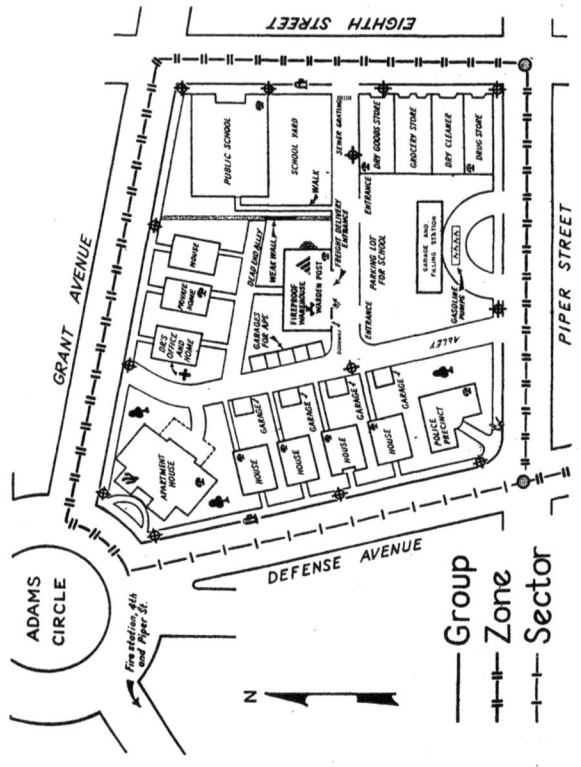

upon the character of the Sector. The usual number is four, which permits a schedule of 6 hours on duty at the post and 18 hours off duty for each Warden during a stand-by period. During an alert, all Wardens report.

At each Post, there will be a Senior Warden and other Wardens assigned as Second Warden,

Third Warden, and Fourth Warden. The Command of the Post will succeed in that order.

In addition, for each building in the Sector housing more than 100 people, in residence or at work, there will be a Building Warden. He will concern himself only with matters pertaining to his own building and will act under the direction of the Senior Warden of the Sector.

In the case of factories large enough to have special Defense Organizations, the remarks as to Building Wardens do not apply. The head of a factory organization has a status similar to a Senior Warden of a Post.

Mark on the map the position of all buildings requiring special Building Wardens.

Equipment of Air Raid Warden's Post.

Post Equipment.

Each Post should be equipped with:
- Desk and sufficient chairs for all personnel.
- Telephone and other communication devices as adopted locally.
- Large flashlights and extra batteries.
- First aid kit and solutions.
- Gas alarm devices.
- Gas detection devices (as available).
- A log book or diary for recording daily occurrences.
- Prescribed report forms.
- Set of required instructions, pamphlets, and texts.
- Typewriter.
- Battery-operated radio.
- Toilet facilities.
- Rope or clothesline, stands and signs for roping off danger areas.

Warden's Equipment.

Each Air Raid Warden should be equipped with:
- Arm band or suitable uniform.
- Steel helmet (when available).
- Gas mask (when available).
- Gas-protective clothing (as available).
- Warden's whistle.
- Heavy work gloves.

Office Lay-out.

Here is a typical office lay-out. Note gas-proof door, sandbags protecting windows from bomb blast, and storage space.

Your Duties as Air Raid Warden.

You have been chosen as Air Raid Warden of your Sector because you are known to be reliable and responsible and because you have the needed qualities to lead, direct, and help the people entrusted to your care.

In your Sector are the homes of some hundreds of your friends and neighbors. It will be your responsibility to see that everything possible is done to protect and safeguard those homes and citizens from the new hazards created by attack from the air or by enemies from within our gates.

As an Air Raid Warden you have specific duties to perform. You must study them, review them, practice them over and over so that you may carry them out in an air raid without failure or error. You must know your Sector as intimately as others know their own homes.

You must know your people well. To them, you are the embodiment of all Civilian Defense. In every way, you must seek to gain their confidence so that in any time of stress you may more easily calm and reassure them and avert panic. As you become better acquainted with the individuals in your Sector, you will learn whom to call upon for informal help at such times.

You are not a policeman nor a fireman nor a doctor, although your duties are related to theirs. As an Air Raid Warden, you have a unique position in American community life. It is a position of leadership and trust that demands an effort not less than your best.

Duties Preliminary to Air Attack.

It is the responsibility of the Senior Warden to see that all Wardens are thoroughly trained and drilled in wartime duties; that they become familiar with every detail of construction and service facilities in the Sector; that they, in turn, train the residents of the Sector in proper conduct or how to help during air raids; and that all signs, special facilities and equipment are procured and kept in a state of readiness.

Training.

A training course covering the subjects listed below will be arranged by the local Defense Organization. The Senior Warden of each Sector is responsible for seeing that all Wardens in his Sector receive this course.

    A. First Aid.—A 10-hour practical course conducted by the American Red Cross.

    B. Methods of Combating Incendiary Bombs.—Lectures and drill as arranged by local Fire Departments under men who have received special training for instructors at the Civilian Defense Schools. Texts will consist of material furnished at Civilian Defense Schools and publications issued or recommended by the Office of Civilian Defense.

    C. Protection Against Gas.—Lectures conducted by specially trained instructors or Reserve Officers. Texts will consist of material furnished at Civilian Defense Schools and publications issued or recommended by the Office of Civilian Defense.

    D. Reports.—A special course in making out, forwarding, and recording reports, arranged by the Chief Warden.

Detailed Knowledge of the Sector.

Under direction of the Senior Warden, a large scale map will be constructed and hung on the wall of the Post to show location of:

A. All buildings, the character of each, and access doors to streets and alleys. Also indicate coal chutes, freight delivery entrances, and in cities, power, steam, or telephone tunnels for use in event of building collapse. (In black.)
B. Fire hydrants, alarm boxes, auxiliary water storage, special fire-fighting equipment, fire stations. (In brown.)
C. Places of special danger, such as oil-storage tanks, filling stations, lumber yards, other highly inflammable materials, firetrap houses, weak walls. (In red.)
D. Emergency places of refuge such as deep, well-protected vaults or cellars, safe inside rooms. (In blue.)
E. Police stations, first-aid posts, hospitals, decontamination stations, road repair stores, and other organized services of Civilian Defense. (By suitable symbol.)

It is not enough to assemble this information on a map. As an Air Raid Warden, you must know it by heart, and be able to find any required position or place in a complete blackout.

Detailed Knowledge of the People.

The people themselves must be studied carefully as to temperament and ability to assist in emergency. The aged and infirm and all children under 5 years of age should be listed and arrangements made to provide them with help if necessary. All persons with special training useful in Civilian Defense should be registered.

All of this information should be recorded in a bound book kept at the Post which will list the following specifically:

Doctors (give specialty).
Nurses (graduate or practical).
Drugstores (nearest, if none in Sector).

Scoutmasters (and number of boys available in troop).
Plant Superintendents.
Building Superintendents (all in Sector).
Building Wardens.
Janitors.
Fire Watchers.
Adjoining Sector Posts.

Standard Symbols for Maps.

Use these standard symbols on all maps—they are intended to make clear the facts you and others will need to know in a hurry.

Symbol	Name	Symbol	Name
	Warden's Post		Bomb Crater
	Fire Watcher's Station		Roped-off Area
	Fire Alarm		Street Car Tracks
	Telephone		Double Tracks
	Air Raid Shelter		Cisterns or Water Reserves
	Gas-Proof Air Raid Shelter		Sector Limits
	Entrance to Shelter		Zone Limits
	Fire Station		Site of Gas Bomb
	Decontamination Squad Depot		Contaminated Area (For large area, blue cross-hatch)
	Repair Squad		Street Lamp
	Casualty Station		Fire Hydrant
	Decontaminating First Aid Station		Sewer Gratings
	Bomb Squad Station		Manhole
	Location of Incident (Show number in center)		Tree
	Demolished Building		Sandbags

Training Selected People.

Certain people in every Sector should be selected and trained to assist the Wardens. The extent of such activity will be determined by the Senior Warden.

Some people will be trained in methods of smothering or extinguishing fire bombs. They may be designated as Fire Watchers and assigned to positions of vantage during an alert to spot and report, then fight incendiaries.

Others may be instructed in how to assist the infirm or sick to positions of greater shelter and in what to do to help prevent or allay panic.

Signs and Guides.

The Warden's Post, places available for group shelter, first-aid posts, and all other Civilian Defense headquarters or depots should be plainly marked. As many directional signs as are necessary to guide strangers should be provided.

The Senior Warden will recommend necessary signs to the Chief Warden through administrative channels. He will report regularly on the condition of curb painting, street lamp and traffic light covers and other protective painting and lighting.

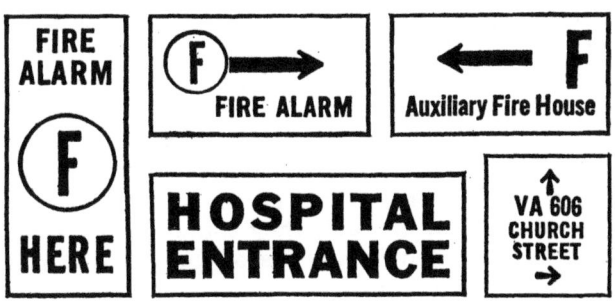

The Air Raid Warden in War.

In time of war or other emergency, think of yourself first as a leader chosen from your neighborhood to do the right thing, with your neighbors and for them. The keynote of your conduct must be courage and presence of mind.

When an "alert" is ordered, go at once to your post, wear your arm band and secure your equipment. Reassure all those you meet and try to persuade them to go about their ordinary tasks until the sirens sound.

The Air Raid Warning.

A far-flung system of Observation Posts, manned by civilians but under direction of the Army Air Corps, reports the presence of enemy planes by telephone to Filter Centers, which report to Information Centers. From these Centers in turn, a spider's web of telephone lines conveys the necessary stand-by and warning signals into each city and town at a point called the Control Center. Your city has a Control Center.

Again the lines spread out, from your Control Center to Message Centers and to such points as hospitals, casualty stations, police stations, and Air Raid Warden's Posts. These lines go also to the alarm sirens that warn everyone to take cover and to the switchboards that control initial phases of the blackout. The initial alert or stand-by will be telephoned to this network and probably broadcast as well.

The sirens, which are operated at the direction of the Control Center, are power sirens or huge electric air horns with great carrying power. To warn of an air raid, they sound with a rising and falling pitch or a series of short blasts, continuing for 2 minutes.

When the planes have passed or been driven off, a single long blast is sounded by the same sirens or horns.

Use of the Warden's Whistle.

The whistle is furnished you to use in drawing attention to your presence in an emergency, not to sound a general warning. Do not run about blowing it to supplement the siren warning.

First Duties Following the Air Raid Warning.

One Warden remains at the Post to receive and forward messages, the others patrol the Sector.

On patrol, your first duty is to clear the streets. People should be told to go to their homes or, if they cannot reach them within 5 minutes, they should be directed to one of the shelter positions in your Sector.

You must see that drivers park their automobiles at curbs, in a double row if necessary, but in such a manner as to leave a passage for fire engines and ambulances. Wide openings must be left opposite fire plugs. The police will enforce this procedure, but Wardens must be alert for any driver abandoning a vehicle without first properly parking it. (Note.—Drivers should leave keys in cars or trucks, since these vehicles may be needed in emergency.)

Horses should be taken out of the shafts and tied to a lamp post where they will get the best protection from walls and buildings.

When the warning sounds after dark, the blackout will be enforced. You will warn householders at once of any light showing and if it is not at once turned out or covered, report the fact to the nearest policeman. The condition of street and traffic lights should be reported. Any shop signs still illuminated should be turned off or reported.

Watchman's lights should be extinguished. (Note.—Where shop signs or watchman's lights are ordinarily left burning after a store is closed, an outside emergency cut-off switch should be installed so that it can be operated by the Air Raid Warden).

You must next be sure that all Fire Watchers are on post and that fire-fighting devices and supplies are ready for use.

When the streets are clear and all lights covered or extinguished, and fire watchers posted, you should take cover in a doorway or other place where you are protected and can observe developments.

If No Bombs Fall.

If no bombs are dropped in your Sector, your duties will be to guide messengers, first-aid, and other parties passing through, to direct fire patrols, to be alert for gas warnings and to prevent people from leaving their homes and shelters. On no account will you leave your Sector to go to the aid of a neighboring Sector.

When Bombs Fall.

As a Warden you must remember that every Warden's first duty is to the Sector as a whole, even before help to individuals in distress. One Warden must always remain on duty at the Post, to act as a guide to arriving services and to answer the telephone and forward messages.

Small Incendiary Bombs.

If small incendiary bombs lodge on top of buildings, your first duty is to warn the occupants and get the Fire Watchers or other trained persons to deal with the bombs. The locations of these bombs should then be reported immediately by telephone to the designated Fire Report Center.

High-Explosive Bombs.

If a bomb explodes, quickly reconnoiter to determine the exact location and extent of damage, then report accurately to the Post or designated Report Center. After this report, give what help and first aid you can to any persons injured by the blast.

If a bomb fails to explode or an explosion cannot be detected above the crash caused by the fall, investigate the bomb at once. It may be a dud, a time bomb, or a gas bomb. As you approach the point of fall, be especially alert for the presence of gas.

If no gas is present, report the location and probable size of the bomb and damage caused by the fall; then, evacuate people in nearby houses and conduct or direct them to other places of shelter. After this, the streets leading to the place of fall should be roped off if there is time. Volunteers may be found for this work.

War Gas.

If gas is detected, sound the gas alarm immediately. In this case nearby residents should be kept from emerging from their homes. Identify the type of gas as accurately as possible and report its presence to the proper Center.

If gas alarms are sounded in neighboring Sectors, first determine in which direction, and how strongly, the wind is blowing. If the alarm comes from the same direction as the wind, move toward it up to the Sector boundary and be ready to sound the alarm at the first betraying odor *but not before*. It is important to avoid spreading a gas alarm any farther than is absolutely necessary.

When low-flying airplanes come over, again be alert for the presence of gas which may be sprayed as well as dropped. If gas spray is detected, sound the gas alarm.

Large Incendiaries and Arson.

If large incendiary bombs are dropped or fires started by enemy agents, their location and character must be reported immediately. Then the fire must be fought with whatever local assistance can be obtained, until fire apparatus arrives.

Where and How To Report.

On the opposite page is a model for reports which you are to make on each air raid incident. As soon as you have the information of an incident, make a report following this form. Include *all* the information which is pertinent.

Whenever possible, make your reports by telephone or such supplementary communication system as is available. However, communication lines may be broken by aerial bombardment and it is highly desirable that messengers be available for emergencies.

If messengers are not assigned by the local Civilian Defense Organization, they may be recruited from the younger members of the population living in your Sector. Either boys or girls over 15 years of age are capable of serving as messengers. Bicycles are desirable aids to normal fast communication by messenger, but they are of little use in a blackout. Messengers should be thoroughly familiar with fastest routes to the Report Centers under blackout conditions.

It is essential that reports be clear and concise. Write them out as you would write a telegram. Always give the number (or other designation) of your own Post first, then give the details as briefly and clearly as possible. Do not use code nor abbreviations unless they are authorized.

WARDEN'S REPORT FORM
(Form of Report to Report Centers)

Commence with the words "AIR RAID DAMAGE."
Designation of REPORTING AGENT: (e. g., Warden's Sector No.)
POSITION of occurrence:
TYPE of bombs: H. E. ☐ Incendiary ☐ Poison gas ☐
Approximate number of CASUALTIES: (if any trapped under wreckage, say so)
If FIRE, say so:
Damage to MAINS: Water ☐ Coal gas ☐ Overhead electric cables ☐ Sewers. ☐
Names of ROADS BLOCKED:
Position of any UNEXPLODED BOMBS:
Time of occurrence (approximate):
Services already ON THE SPOT or COMING:
Remarks:
Finish with the words "MESSAGE ENDS."

See that each report you send contains all the pertinent information included in the table above. Do not use this page for reports —it is a check-list to help you make sure you have included everything.

Note Here Where To Send Reports.

Report Bomb Explosions to _____
_____ Telephone _____
Report Unexploded Bombs to _____
_____ Telephone _____
Report Gas Bombs to _____
_____ Telephone _____
Report Fire Bombs to _____
_____ Telephone _____
Nearest Police Station _____
_____ Telephone _____
Nearest Fire Station _____
_____ Telephone _____
Nearest Decontamination Station (for Persons)___
_____ Telephone _____
Nearest Casualty Station _____
_____ Telephone _____
Nearest Hospital _____
_____ Telephone _____
Nearest Decontamination Squad Depot _____
_____ Telephone _____
Location and Addresses of Posts in Adjoining Sectors:
_____ Telephone _____
_____ Telephone _____
_____ Telephone _____
_____ Telephone _____

Final Reports.

In addition to the immediate reports of an air raid incident, a final report must be made when an incident is closed. This will be prepared by the Warden in charge of action in the case for transmission by the Senior Warden to his superiors.

Keeping the Log.

The events of each day should be kept in the log book in diary form. Write up all events clearly and concisely.

After preliminary Post Organization is completed, the Senior Warden should assemble all Wardens at least once a week, read the log, and cause to be entered in the record book and on the Sector map any important changes or additions.

Fire Watchers.

Combating incendiary bombs is everyone's duty, yet not all individuals can cope with the intense heat, nor do all have the necessary physical stamina. As a practical measure, the most stalwart persons in each block or apartment should be chosen for training in the methods of combating fire bombs, particularly the light magnesium bombs. For training purposes, probably a bomb will have to be simulated by burning a rolled-up newspaper or some similar device. Training should be given the selected individuals in both the sand method (snuffing) and water spray method (accelerating). When they have shown satisfactory aptitude, they may be enrolled in the Civilian Defense forces as Fire Watchers and assigned to regular posts of vantage.

Your Civilian Defense Council will issue to those accepted for enrollment arm bands, identification cards, and handbooks.

Fire Watchers take up their stations only after an air raid alarm sounds. From these positions, all roof areas must be watched. The Post map should be marked with a red triangle at the points where Fire Watchers are stationed. Fire

Watchers' duties are described in a separate handbook to be issued soon by the U. S. Office of Civilian Defense.

Place watchers on high places, standpipes, steeples, etc., so that all roof areas can be watched with the fewest posts.

Air Raid Wardens of Post No. _____
City of _____, *State of* _____

---

1. Senior Warden _____

BUSINESS ADDRESS — TELEPHONE

HOME ADDRESS — TELEPHONE

2. Second Warden _____

BUSINESS ADDRESS — TELEPHONE

HOME ADDRESS — TELEPHONE

3. Third Warden _____

BUSINESS ADDRESS — TELEPHONE

HOME ADDRESS — TELEPHONE

4. Fourth Warden _____

BUSINESS ADDRESS — TELEPHONE

HOME ADDRESS — TELEPHONE

Building Wardens:
  (1) Building address _____
      Name of warden _____
                      TELEPHONE
  (2) Building address _____
      Name of warden _____
                      TELEPHONE

Handicapped People—Deaf and Blind

The Warden has a special responsibility for every *deaf* and *blind* person in his Sector.

Find out who and where they are. Find out who will be responsible *at all times* for letting deaf people know that there is an air-raid alarm. Find out who will be responsible *at all times* for letting blind people know that a blackout is on or ordered, who will positively see that their lights are out, and who will take care of getting them into refuge rooms if necessary.

It is hoped that all handicapped persons can be evacuated to safe areas in advance of the threat on the neighborhoods where they live; however, *it is up to the Warden* to take care of them, especially, or see that some reliable person does take care of them, whatever happens.

"If I were a Warden"

My first job would be to know everyone and every house and every street and lamp-post and manhole and gas shut-off and electrical connection in my sector; to know what people could do, and to put them to work ready to do it; to see that attics were cleaned out, and made fire-resisting; to see that every house had garden hose with spray and jet nozzle, buckets, emergency water-supply, and a few simple tools.

I would want them to know me, have confidence in me, and be prepared to work with me and the other members of the U. S. Citizens' Defense Corps.

I would want to know how to do a lot of things myself; put out incendiary bombs; direct emergency vehicles; defend myself against gas; make a map of my sector; use the telephone on emergency calls; know where the other services (auxiliary fire, auxiliary police, bomb squads, repair squads, decontamination squads, etc.) were located;

especially to know where, when, and how to report a "bomb incident."

When a blackout was ordered, I would expect to see that it was complete, and that blackout orders were complied with. I would warn people, who showed lights, to extinguish or cover them instantly; and if they failed or refused to do so, I would get a regular or auxiliary police officer to enforce the blackout.

If and when an air-raid alarm were given, I would have two principal duties right off: (1) to get people into shelter, and (2) to clear the streets seeing that cars were parked and that a clear way was left for emergency vehicles.

I would have chosen and trained fire watchers; in the event of bombing; I would want to see that the fire watchers man their posts, and know how, what, when, and where to report.

Should bombs fall in my sector, I would go to the scene of the incident, estimate damage, report it, and take charge as "incident officer" if I were the senior officer present.

I would expect to direct the emergency vehicles as to the best way to get to the incident. I would expect to take charge of property from bombed premises, for claiming later by the owners.

I would, of course, expect to quiet the fears of people who showed signs of becoming panic-stricken.

I would expect to be a sort of "noncommissioned officer" for the civilian populace.

John Strachey says of the English Wardens, "their quietness has echoed around the world; their ordinariness has become a flag; their kindness has become a rock; their courage has become an avalanche. In their amusement, Empires melt." That would be my ideal if I were a warden.

THE WARDEN REPORTS

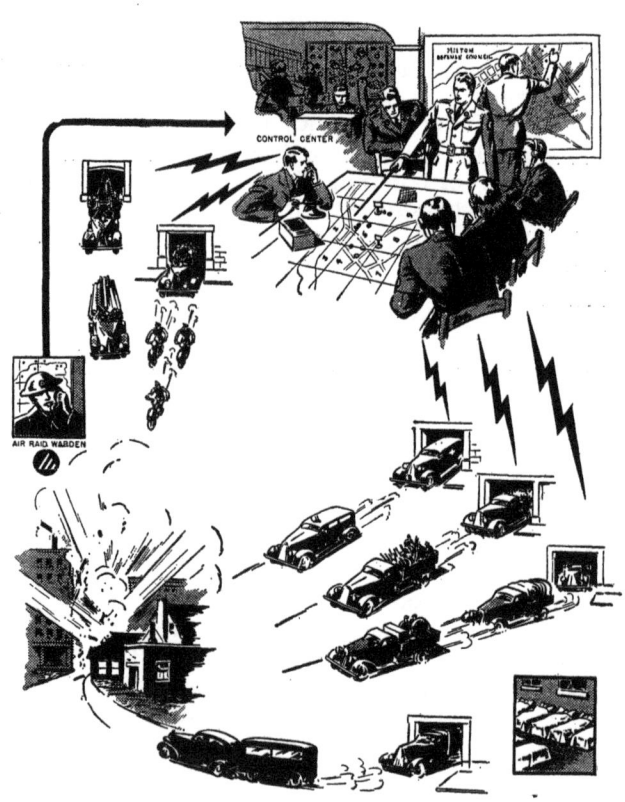

Despite all the efforts of active defense, a bomber has reached its objective and the first bombs fall. The nearest warden at once inspects the damage, and telephones his report, through channels, to the Control Center.

As reports are assembled and plotted on the Control Map, the Commander of the Local Citizens Defense Corps sends his forces into action. Regular and Auxiliary Fire Forces are dispatched to the fires started by incendiary bombs. Rescue Squads and First Aid Parties speed to help the trapped and injured; Demolition and Clearance Squads, followed by the Road Repair Crews, clear away the rubble and reopen the streets to traffic.

Close in their wake come those who will feed and find beds for families made homeless in the attack.

To be a modern minute man you need organization and training.

This Page Is for Warden's Notes

This Page Is for Warden's Notes

This Page Is for Warden's Notes

BLACKOUTS

Blackouts are ordered only on the authority of the War Department. A blackout may be ordered during any period when hostile forces are believed to be in the vicinity, whether or not enemy airplanes have been sighted.

"Blacking Out" a city means that light sources must be so hidden or dimmed that an enemy bomber will have difficulty in finding the target and lack aiming points such as main street intersections. Following are the general plans used.

Street Lights. These are fitted with low-watt bulbs and covers that diffuse the light.

Automobiles. Headlights must be covered except for a small pair of slits and hooded.

Traffic Lights. Are treated the same way as automobile headlights.

Buildings. Windows and doors must be covered with opaque materials. Paint on the glass, heavy curtains, light "baffles" or screens are some of the ways. No cracks of light must show.

Aids to Seeing. Since people have to move about during a blackout, the lack of light may be somewhat offset and safety promoted by—

1. Painting curbs, trees, poles and hydrants with white paint. There is a luminous paint, also, that gives off a faint blue light quite visible in total darkness.

2. Painting signs of luminous paint or making them of fluorescent material on which shines ultra-violet or "black" light or installing dimly lighted signs with horizontal screens to diffuse the light.

3. Painting white fenders and stripes around automobiles.

Members of the Citizens' Defense Corps who have outside duties during a blackout can be identified more easily if they wear a white cap or white-painted helmet; also a white belt fitted with crossed straps over the shoulders.

Individual Conduct During a Blackout.

Observe traffic rules. Keep to the right and remember the man or vehicle approaching *from* your right *has* the right of way.

If you must smoke, go into a hallway or covered place to strike the match. No smoking in the open is an even better rule. Make all crossings at intersections. It is hard for a driver to see you.

Be sure that everyone you know is acquainted with these simple rules.

DO NOT run when air raid warnings sound after dark during blackouts.

Use your flashlight as little as possible, if at all. Never point it upward.

Curb edges and direction signs painted white will help you find your way.

Keep pets on leash if you take them out after dark.

If an air raid warning sounds, get under cover, you may be hit by shell fragments.

If you don't know the neighborhood the first policeman or warden will tell you where to go

When an observer sights a group of hostile planes, he picks up his telephone (1) and says *Army Flash*. The Central Operator (2) at once connects him with the assigned Filter Center (3) to which he reports the type of planes, number, height, and direction of flight. When several reports agree, watchers transmit the data to an Information Center (4) where developments over a large area are plotted on a huge map.

Watching the map, Air Corps officers order interceptor planes into the air, (5) direct them to contact with the enemy; another officer notes the cities threatened and flashes a yellow, blue, or red alarm, according to the degree of danger, to the proper Warning District Center (6).

At this point, Civilian Defense takes over from the Air Corps, telephones the warnings to Control Centers (7) within the Warning District. And here the Commander of the local Citizens' Defense Corps orders the alert, has the public warning sounded usually short blasts on air horns, power horns or steam whistles or on the wailing sirens— and if the bombers arrive overhead, directs the operation of passive defense. Learn the air raid warning for your city.

FLASH

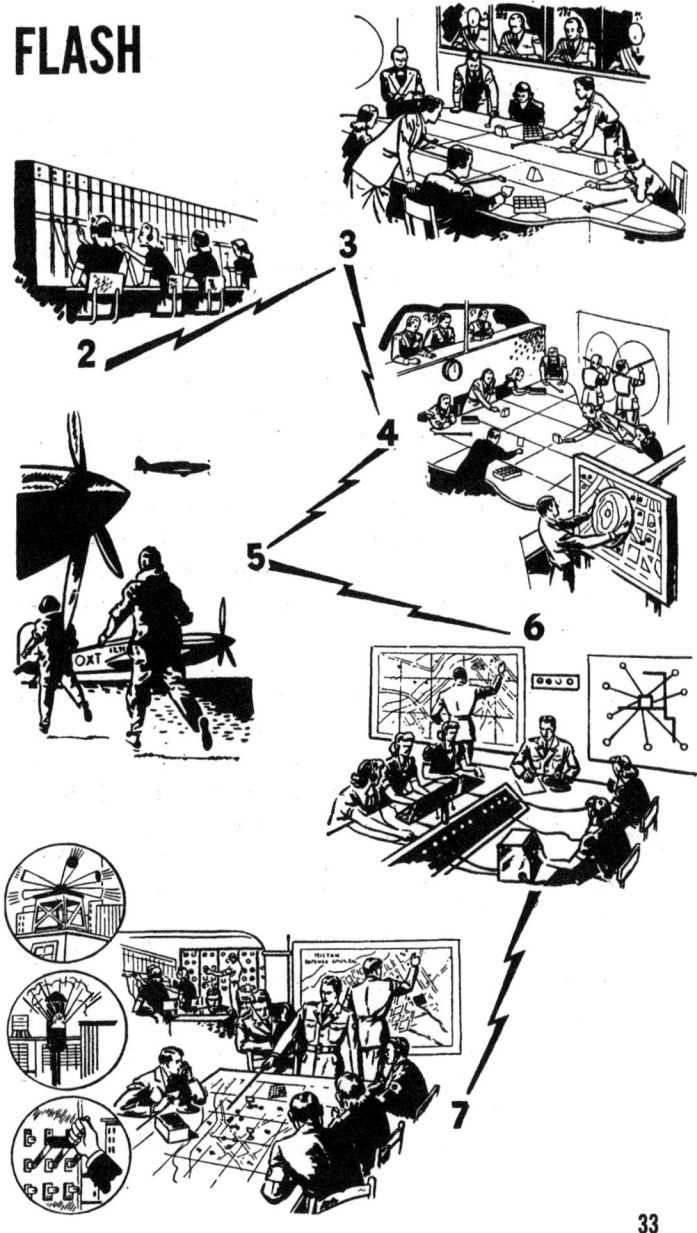

The Refuge Room

WHAT TO DO IN AN AIR RAID

At the yellow warning, if you are not already on duty, you will be summoned to your post and will carry out orders until relieved. However, here are the rules for those who do not have assigned duties when the air raid warning comes. Memorize them carefully so that you can in turn instruct others. Here is what to tell them:

1. If away from home, seek the nearest shelter. Get off the street.

2. If you are driving, first park your car at the curb; be sure all lights are shut off.

3. If you are at home, send the others to the refuge room. This should be a comfortable place with as little window exposure as possible, equipped with drinking water, things to read, toilet facilities, a flashlight, a portable radio, a sturdy table, and food if you like.

4. Turn off all gas stove burners but leave pilot lights, water heaters and furnaces alone. Leave electricity and water on. Fill some large containers or a bathtub with water.

5. Check up on blackout arrangements. Don't let a crack of light show to the outside.

6. See that everyone's eyeglasses and dentures are in the refuge room. There should be additional warm garments for everyone, too.

7. Keep out of line of windows. Fragments and glass splinters cause most casualties.

8. If bombs fall nearby, get under a heavy table, an overturned davenport.

9. Don't rush out when the "all clear" signal sounds. Maintain the blackout. The Raiders may return.

10. Otherwise, keep cool; be sensible and set an example to others.

FIRE DEFENSE

It will be very difficult to fight a magnesium bomb unless some work is done before the attack

All furniture trunks and junk of all kinds should be removed from attic or top floor!

Roof beams joists and studs can be treated to resist flame — giving more time to reach the bomb

Paint does no good! A heavy coat of ordinary whitewash helps some

HOW THE MAGNESIUM BOMB WORKS

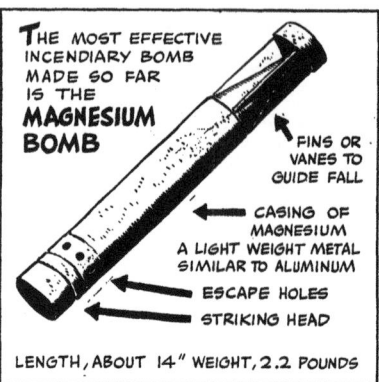

The most effective incendiary bomb made so far is the **MAGNESIUM BOMB**

← FINS OR VANES TO GUIDE FALL
← CASING OF MAGNESIUM A LIGHT WEIGHT METAL SIMILAR TO ALUMINUM
← ESCAPE HOLES
← STRIKING HEAD

LENGTH, ABOUT 14" WEIGHT, 2.2 POUNDS

A large bomber can carry 1000 such bombs!

They are usually released 20 to 50 at a time, spread like shot before striking.

Dropped from a height of 20,000 feet, they develop enough force to penetrate an average roof...

...thus, they usually start burning in a top story or attic

The thermite filling of iron oxide and finely divided aluminum is then ignited and develops a fierce heat of **OVER 4500 DEGREES!**

The flame roars out of the escape holes.

The magnesium casing catches fire, with a sputtering action...

...flaming molten metal is thrown about and surrounding inflammable material catches fire

If not quickly quenched, the bomb will burn through the floor, setting additional fires on the floor below...

BUT, WITH PROMPT ACTION AND SIMPLE TOOLS, A MAGNESIUM BOMB CAN BE QUENCHED!

CONTROLLING WITH WATER

To fight a bomb with water, you need two men and special equipment. Remember, you can't put out the bomb — you feed it water, to BURN OUT!

One man pumps 80 strokes a minute to keep a strong enough pressure to throw a jet 30 feet, as spray, 15 feet. One man fights the fire.

You use up a bucket in 1½ minutes

Special double action pump with 30 feet of hose and special nozzle needed.

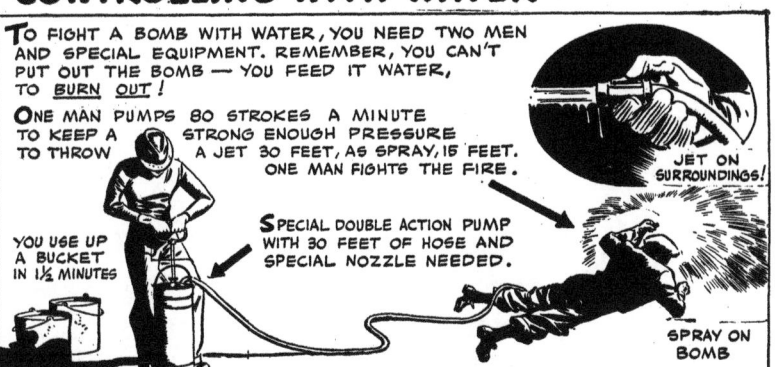

JET ON SURROUNDINGS!

SPRAY ON BOMB

A third person is most useful to check other points for flame, replenish water and relieve pumper.

Ample storage of water should be provided in advance, as water mains may be broken by high explosives and pressure lost! Fill the tub, extra pails and don't forget in a pinch — the contents of hot water or heating boilers!

NEVER THROW THE CONTENTS OF A WATER PAIL ON A BOMB!

...IT WILL SCATTER WITH EXPLOSIVE VIOLENCE!

If control of the bomb seems doubtful, have an alarm turned in, but continue fighting the bomb until help arrives or supplies are exhausted!

1. LEARN **NOW** HOW TO CALL
2. LEARN **NOW** LOCATION OF NEAREST ALARM...

CONTROLLING WITH SAND

APPROACH THE BOMB IN A CROUCHING OR CRAWLING POSITION. PLACE THE SAND BUCKET, UPSET, TO ALLOW A FULL-ARM SWING TOWARD THE BOMB.

TRY TO COVER THE BOMB WITH DRY SAND, TO CONFINE IT'S ACTION, SO THAT YOU CAN GET NEAR ENOUGH TO SCOOP IT UP ON THE SHOVEL

WHEN THE BOMB IS UNDER FAIR CONTROL, SCOOP IT UP ON THE SHOVEL, FIRST RIGHTING THE BUCKET, BUT LEAVING SOME SAND IN THE BOTTOM...

...IF THE BOMB CAN BE DROPPED FROM A WINDOW TO SOME PLACE WHERE IT CAN BURN OUT WITHOUT HARM —

GET RID OF IT THAT WAY!

...OTHERWISE, PUT IT IN THE BUCKET ON TOP OF SAND, COVER IT WITH MORE SAND...

...THEN, HOLDING THE BUCKET ON THE SHOVEL, CARRY IT OUT OF THE HOUSE...

ABOUT FIRE EXTINGUISHERS

Many houses and public buildings have fire extinguishers. They will be as useful as ever in putting out fires caused by an incendiary bomb. For putting out the bomb itself, the extinguisher may not be suitable.

Read the label. If it says that the contents include CARBON TETRACHLORIDE, it cannot under any circumstances be used on a magnesium bomb. It is not only ineffective, it may cause dangerous gas to be generated. After the bomb is burnt out, use it on any remaining fire.

All water-type extinguishers are suitable. If the label says SODA-ACID, that's simply a means of creating pressure in the extinguisher. Turn it upside down, use it. You can get a spray effect by putting the thumb over the nozzle, use the jet on surrounding fires. However, *one extinguisher is not enough to burn out a magnesium bomb*. And you cannot refill the extinguisher.

It is best to have sand or pump-bucket equipment handy, use them on the bomb, and save the extinguishers for resulting fires.

A foam extinguisher will also help to control a bomb, but one extinguisher load will not finish the job.

See that the extinguishers you know about are ready for use.

CHEMICAL WARFARE AGENTS
REFERENCE AND TRAINING CHART

LEGEND: HOSPITAL CASE | FIRST AID STATION | LUNG PROTECTION NEEDED | COMPLETE PROTECTION NEEDED

The importance of proper first aid for gas victims cannot be overemphasized. The following are general rules which apply in all cases.

A. Act promptly and quietly; be calm.
B. Put a gas mask on the patient if gas is still present or, if he has a mask on, check to see that this is properly adjusted. If a mask is not available, wet a handkerchief or other cloth and have him breathe through it.
C. Keep the patient at absolute rest; loosen clothing to facilitate breathing.
D. Remove the patient to a gas-free place as soon as possible.
E. Summon medical aid promptly; if possible, send the victim to a hospital.
F. Do not permit the patient to smoke, as this causes coughing and, hence, exertion.

CLASS	NAMES AND SYMBOLS	FORM	ODOR	PERSISTENCE	TACTICAL CLASS	PROTECTION	FIRST AID (After removal from gassed area)	PHYSIOLOGICAL EFFECT
VESICANTS	MUSTARD $S(CH_2CH_2)_2Cl_2$ DI-CHLORETHYL SULFIDE	LIQUID AND VAPOR	Garlic, Horseradish, Mustard	One day to one week. Longer if dry or cold.			Undress; remove liquid mustard with protective ointment, bleach paste, or kerosene; bathe, wash eyes and nose with soda solution.	Delayed effect. Burns skin or membrane. Inflammation respiratory tract, leading to pneumonia. Eye irritation, conjunctivitis.
VESICANTS	LEWISITE $CHCCH-AsCl_2$ CHLORVINYL-DICHLORARSINE	LIQUID AND VAPOR	Geraniums	One day to one week. Longer if dry or cold.			Undress; remove liquid Lewisite with hydrogen peroxide, lye in glycerine, or kerosene; bathe; wash eyes and nose with soda. Rest.—Doctor.	Burning or irritation of eyes, nasal passages, respiratory tract, skin. Arsenical poison.
LUNG IRRITANTS	CHLORPICRIN CCl_3NO_2 NITROCHLOROFORM	GAS	Flypaper, anise	Open 6 hours. Woods 12 hours.			Wash eyes, keep quiet and warm. Do not use bandages.	Causes severe coughing, crying, vomiting.
LUNG IRRITANTS	DIPHOSGENE $ClCOOC-Cl_3$ TRICHLOROMETHYL, CHLOROFORMATE	GAS	Ensilage, Hay(?)	30 minutes.			Keep quiet and warm. Give coffee as a stimulant.	Causes coughing, breathing hurts, eyes water, toxic.
LUNG IRRITANTS	PHOSGENE $COCl_2$ CARBONYL CHLORIDE	GAS	Musty hay, Green corn	10 to 30 minutes.			Keep quiet and warm, bed rest. Coffee as a stimulant. Loosen clothing. No alcohol or cigarettes.	Irritation of lungs, occasional vomiting, tears in eyes, dazed feeling. Occasionally symptoms delayed. Later, collapse, heart failure.
LACRIMATORS	CLORACETOPHENONE $C_6H_5CO-CH_2Cl$	GAS	Apple blossoms	10 minutes.			Wash eyes with cold water or boric acid solution. Do not bandage. Face wind. For skin, sodium sulphite solution.	Makes eyes smart. Shut tightly. Tears flow. Temporary.
LACRIMATORS	BROMBENZYLCYANIDE $C_6H_5CH-BrCN$	GAS	Sour fruit	Several days. (Weeks in winter.)			Wash eyes with boric acid. Do not bandage.	Eyes smart, shut, tears flow. Effect lasts some time. Headache.
STERNUTATORS	ADAMSITE $(C_6H_4)_2=NHAsCl$ DIPHENYLAMINECHLORARSINE	GAS	Coal Smoke	10 minutes.			Keep quiet and warm. Loosen clothing. Reassure. Spray nose with neo-synephrin or sniff bleaching powder. Aspirin for headache.	Causes sneezing, sick depressed feeling, headache.
STERNUTATORS	DIPHENYLCHLORARSINE $(C_6H_5)_2-AsCl$	SMOKE	Shoe Polish	Summer 10 minutes.			Remove to pure air, keep quiet. Sniff chlorine from bleaching powder bottle.	Causes sick feeling and headache.

40

WAR GASES

General Notes.

War "Gases," or chemical agents used to produce casualties, are surprise weapons. As this is written, they have not been used against the British or others trained to protect themselves. They have been used against the Ethiopians and the Chinese.

A gas-tight room suitably located offers fair protection against any probable concentration of war gas in a city. For those whose duties take them into the streets a gas mask offers full protection against all but the "blister gases" (liquid vesicants). To enter areas where mustard or lewisite is present, full protective clothing is needed.

War gases may be dropped in bombs or simple containers and liquid vesicants may also be sprayed by airplanes.

The gas warning is a "percussion sound"— that is, bells, drums, hand rattles, rapidly struck resonant objects of any kind. If the presence of gas is suspected, report to the nearest warden. Do not shout if distant gas alarms are heard. The danger is local and the spreading of an alarm must be left to the wardens.

The notes on the following pages are simply for reference for those who have received instruction in protection against gas. Reading them will not by itself make you an expert in gas defense.

THE GAS-TIGHT ROOM

War gases hug the ground, flow into cellars and basements. Upper floors of a dwelling are away from dangerous concentrations. If all openings and cracks are closed, a room three stories from the ground will offer good protection against war gases.

To stop cracks and small openings, tape of various kinds may be used. A mush made by soaking newspapers in water or patching plaster may be used for caulking larger openings. A piece of wall board, nails and caulking material may be kept handy to cover a window broken by the blast of high explosives.

One door may be used as an entrance by fastening over it a blanket in such a way as to seal it tightly when no one is going in or out. If soaked in oil to close the air spaces, the blanket is more effective.

Store necessary supplies in such a room—food, water, chairs, a battery-operated radio, flashlight and by all means provide some sort of toilet facilities use it as the refuge room.

Allow 20 square feet of floor space for each person who is to occupy an average room with a ceiling nine feet high. This will give enough air to occupy the room 10 hours.

The illustration shows where to stop up cracks, how to hang the blanket at the entrance door.

"Blister Gases" and Decontamination.

Lewisite and mustard "gas" are liquids in the normal state. They give off a dangerous vapor that acts as a war gas and unless chemically neutralized may persist for a week, contaminating the air for a considerable distance down wind.

Full protection against these chemical agents is afforded by gas-proof clothing, covering the wearer from top to toe and tightened at wrists and ankles. The greatest care must be used in undressing after exposure to lewisite or mustard and this is done at personnel decontamination stations, where vesicant casualties are also taken for first aid.

Decontamination of streets, walls, and buildings is effected principally by means of chloride of lime (bleaching powder) freshly mixed with earth and water as a slurry or paste. It must be thoroughly worked into cracks and crevices and the resulting product flushed away. This work is done by the decontamination squads.

The liquid vesicants are very penetrating and ordinary shoes or clothing offer no protection. Do not go into the streets after a gas alarm has been sounded except on direction of the Warden.

RANK DESIGNATION	▲	▲▲	▲▲▲	◁	◁◁	◁◁◁	★	★★	★★★	★★★★
AIR RAID WARDEN	FIRST CLASS	SENIOR OR SECTOR WARDEN	ZONE LEADER	GROUP LEADER	CHIEF WARDEN	STATE WARDEN	NO OTHER RANKS			
AUXILIARY FIREMEN	"	SQUAD LEADER	PLATOON LEADER	COMPANY LEADER	FIRE CHIEF	STATE FIRE COORDINATOR	NO OTHER RANKS			
AUXILIARY POLICEMEN	"	"	"	"	CHIEF OF POLICE	NO OTHER RANKS				
BOMB SQUADS	"	"	NONE	"	"	NO OTHER RANKS				
RESCUE SQUADS	"	"	DEPOT LEADER	"	FIRE CHIEF	NO OTHER RANKS				
MEDICAL FIELD UNITS	"	TEAM LEADER	SQUAD LEADER	UNIT LEADER	CHIEF OF E.M.S.	STATE MEDICAL DIRECTOR	NO OTHER RANKS			
MEDICAL AUXILIARIES (stretcher teams)	"	" ✱	" ✱	NO OTHER RANKS						
NURSES' AIDES	NO RANK DESIGNATIONS									
EMERGENCY FOOD AND HOUSING	FIRST CLASS	UNIT LEADER	DEPOT LEADER	COMPANY LEADER	CHIEF WARDEN	NO OTHER RANKS				
DRIVERS UNITS	"	CONVOY LEADER	"	"	NO OTHER RANKS					
MESSENGERS	"	SENIOR MESSENGER	PLATOON LEADER	"	NO OTHER RANKS					
ROAD REPAIR CREWS	"	CREW LEADER	DEPOT LEADER	"						
DEMOLITION AND CLEAR.	"	"	"	"	CHIEF OF EMER. WORK S.	NO OTHER RANKS				
DECONTAMINATION SQUADS	"	SQUAD LEADER	STATION LEADER	"						
FIRE WATCHERS	"	NO OTHER RANKS								
REPAIR CREWS	"	CREW LEADER	SERVICE LEADER	NONE	CHIEF OF UTILITIES	NO OTHER RANKS				
LOCAL STAFF	"	AS REQUIRED			CONTROLLER	COMMANDER	COORDINATOR	NO OTHER RANKS		
STATE STAFF	"	AS REQUIRED			AS DESIGNATED	AS DESIGNATED	ASST. COORDINATOR	COORDINATOR	NO OTHER RANKS	
U.S. STAFF	"	AS REQUIRED				AS DESIGNATED	AS DESIGNATED	AS DESIGNATED	REGION DIRECTOR PRINCIPAL ASST'S	U.S. DIRECTOR
EQUIVALENT ARMY TERM	PVT. 1st CLASS	NON-COMM. OFF.	LIEUTENANT	CAPTAIN	MAJOR	COLONEL	BRIG. GEN.	MAJ. GEN.	LIEUT. GEN.	GENERAL

✱ASSIGNED BY RED CROSS TO CHIEF OF EMERGENCY MEDICAL SERVICE.

CITIZENS' DEFENSE CORPS

The team of trained civilian services organized to operate the passive defense is known as the Citizens' Defense Corps. It includes regular forces of the city—police, firemen, welfare workers, sanitation men—as well as volunteers. It operates as a unit under the local Defense Coordinator.

Staff.

The Citizens' Defense Corps is headed by a Commander assisted by a staff. His second in command is the Executive Officer. There are others who operate the control center and the communications, account for personnel and property and assign transportation. The Chiefs of the Fire and Police Departments assist him in the passive defense. There is a Chief Air Raid Warden, a Chief of Emergency Medical Services, and others who control groups of the enrolled volunteers. Learn the organization of the Citizens' Defense Corps in your community.

Enrolled Volunteer Services of The Citizens' Defense Corps.

Air Raid Wardens are in complete charge of a sector containing the homes of about 500 people. To them the warden is the embodiment of all Civilian Defense.

Auxiliary Firemen assist the regular fire-fighting forces.

Auxiliary Policemen assist the police department in enforcing blackout restrictions, in traffic control, and in guard duties.

Bomb Squads are specially trained squads of police to handle and dispose of time bombs and duds.

Rescue Squads are trained crews of about 10 men each with special equipment to rescue the injured from debris.

Medical Forces consist of first-aid parties and stretcher squads and personnel at casualty clearing stations. Members of these forces are doctors, trained nurses, and assistants.

Nurses' Aides assist nurses. They have special Red Cross Training.

Emergency Food and Housing Corps members provide welfare services to the needy and homeless.

Drivers Units consist of emergency drivers of vehicles used by the Civilian Defense services.

Messengers carry supplies, dispatches, and messages wherever needed.

Road Repair Crews restore normal flow of traffic as quickly as possible. Utility repair men work with these crews and with demolition squads.

Demolition and Clearance Crews remove rubble, fill bomb craters, and remove unsafe walls or parts of buildings.

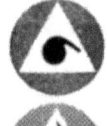
Decontamination squad members are specially trained to treat clothing and equipment as well as streets and walls contaminated by war gas.

Fire Watchers must spot and combat incendiary bombs.

A MANUAL OF DRILL
для
CITIZENS' DEFENSE CORPS

Adapted from the Basic Field Manual of the United States Army

Basic drill is required of a volunteer for award of the insigne. Drill for units of the Citizens' Defense Corps, moreover, is recommended as it helps to coordinate the work of individuals under a single command. The purposes of drill are:

1 To enable a leader to move his unit from one place to another in an orderly manner.

2 To aid in disciplinary training by instilling habits of precision and response to the leader's orders.

3 To provide a means, through ceremonies, of enhancing the morale; develop a spirit of cohesion; and give an interesting spectacle to the public.

4 To give leaders practical training in commanding volunteers.

Drills should be frequent, intensive, and of short duration.

General.

A normal squad of volunteers contains 12 men or 12 women, all of one service. It consists of a leader, an assistant leader, and other personnel. As far as practicable, the squad is kept intact. The usual formation of the squad is a single rank or single file. This permits variations in the number of men composing the squad.

To Form the Squad.

The command is; FALL IN. At the command FALL IN the squad forms in line as shown. Squad leader on the squad's extreme right, assistant leader on the squad's extreme left.

To secure uniformity, the tallest leader is put in charge of the first squad, the second tallest in charge of the second squad, etc. Assistant

Fig. I—A Squad in Line

leaders are similarly arranged. Other volunteers are placed according to height beginning with the tallest being placed next to the leader.

On falling in, each man except the one on the left extends his left arm laterally at shoulder height, palm of the hand down, fingers extended and joined. Each man, except the one on the right, turns his head and eyes to the right and places himself in line so that his right shoulder touches lightly the tips of the fingers of the man on his right. As soon as proper intervals have been obtained, each man comes to attention, drops his arm smartly to his side and turns his head to

Fig. II—A Volunteer at Attention

the front, heels are together, feet forming a right angle; knees are straight without stiffness, hips level and drawn back slightly, body erect and resting equally on hips, chest lifted and arched, shoulders square and falling equally. Arms hang straight down without stiffness with the back of the hands out, fingers held naturally. Head erect and squarely to the front, chin drawn in so that the axis of the head and neck is vertical, eyes straight to the front. The weight of the body rests equally on the heels and the balls of the feet. In assuming the position of attention the heels are brought together smartly and audibly.

(Leaders and assistant leaders will be appointed under authority defined by the Chief of the Service of which the squad forms a part.

To Form at Close Intervals.

The commands are: At Close Interval, FALL IN. At the command FALL IN, the volunteers fall in as described above, except that close intervals are obtained by placing the left hands on the hips. In this position the heel of the palm of the hand rests on the hip, the fingers and thumb are extended and joined, and the elbow is in the plane of the body.

Fig. III—A Volunteer Falling in at Close Interval

To Aline the Squad.

If in line, the commands are: Dress Right, DRESS, Ready, Front. At the command DRESS, each man except the one on the left extends his left arm (or if at close interval, places his left hand upon his hip), and all aline themselves to the right. The instructor places himself on the right flank one pace from and in prolongation of the line and facing down the line. From this position he verifies the alinement of the men, ordering individual men to move forward or back as is necessary. Having checked the alinement, he faces to the right in marching and moves three paces forward, halts, faces to the left and commands: Ready, FRONT. At the command FRONT, arms are dropped quietly and smartly to the sides and heads turned to the front.

Rests.

Being at a halt the commands are: FALL OUT, REST, AT EASE, and PARADE REST.

At the command FALL OUT, volunteers leave the ranks but are required to remain in the immediate vicinity.

At the command REST, one foot is kept in place. Silence and immobility are not required.

At the command AT EASE the right foot is

kept in place. Silence but not immobility is required.

At the command of execution **REST** of Parade **REST**, move the left foot smartly 12 inches to the left of the right foot keeping the legs straight so that the weight of the body rests equally on both feet. At the same time, clasp the hands behind the back, palms to the rear, thumb and fingers of the right hand clasping the left thumb without constraint; preserving silence and immobility.

Being at any of the rests except **FALL OUT**, to resume the position of Attention, the commands are Squad (or other unit being commanded) **ATTENTION**. At the command **ATTENTION** take that position in your squad.

Eyes right (left).

The commands are: Eyes (Preliminary Command), RIGHT (Command of Execution) (LEFT) Ready FRONT! At the command **RIGHT**, each man turns his head and eyes to the right. At the command **FRONT** the head and eyes are turned to the front.

Facings.

(All Facings are executed at the halt.)

To the flank.—The commands are Right (Left) FACE. At the command FACE, slightly raise the left heel and the right toe: Face to the right, turning on the right heel, assisted by a slight pressure on the ball of the left foot. Next, place the left foot beside the right. Exercise Left FACE on the left heel in a corresponding manner.

To the rear.—The commands are: About FACE. At the command FACE, carry the toe of the right foot a half-foot length to the rear and slightly to the left of the left heel without changing

Fig. IV—Executing Right FACE

the position of the left foot; weight of the body mainly on the heel of the left foot; right leg straight without stiffness. (TWO) Face to the rear turning to the right on the left heel and on the ball of the right foot, place the right heel beside the left.

Steps and Marchings.

All steps and marchings executed from the halt, except right step, begin with the left foot.

Quick Time: Being at a halt, to march forward in quick time, the commands are: Forward MARCH. At the command Forward, shift the weight of the body to the right leg without perceptible movement. At the command MARCH, step off smartly with the left foot and continue the march with steps taken straight forward without stiffness or exaggeration of movements. Swing the arms easily in their natural arcs, 6 inches to the front and 3 inches to the rear of the body. To halt when marching in quick time, the commands are: Squad HALT. At the command HALT, given as either foot strikes the ground, execute the halt in two counts by advancing and planting the other foot and then bringing up the foot in rear.

To Mark Time the commands are; Mark-Time, MARCH.

Being in march at the command MARCH, given as either foot strikes the ground, advance and plant the other foot, bring up the foot in rear, placing it so that both heels are on line and continue the cadence by alternately raising and planting each foot. The feet are raised 2 inches from the ground.

Being at a halt, at the command MARCH, raise and plant first the left then the right as prescribed above.

The halt is executed from mark time as from quick time.

Half Step.—The commands are: Half Step MARCH. At the command MARCH, take steps of 15 inches in quick time. To resume the full step from the half step or mark time the commands are: Forward MARCH.

Side Step.—Being at a halt the commands are: Right (Left) Step MARCH. At the command MARCH, carry the right foot 12 inches to the right, place the left foot beside the right, left knee straight. Continue the cadence of quick time. (The side step is executed in quick time from the halt and for short distances only.)

Back Step.—Being at a halt the commands are, Backward MARCH. At the command MARCH, take steps, beginning with the left foot, 15 inches straight to the rear.

To March to the Flank.—Being in march the commands are: By The Right (Left) Flank—MARCH. At the command MARCH, given as the right (left) foot strikes the ground, advance and plant the left (right) foot, then face to the right (left) in marching and step off in the new direction.

Oblique March.—Being in march the commands are Right (Left) Oblique—MARCH. At the command MARCH, given as the right (left) foot strikes the ground, advance and plant the left (right) foot, then face to the right (left) oblique in marching and step off in the new direction.

To resume the original direction, the commands are—Forward, MARCH. At the command MARCH each individual faces half left (right) in marching then moves straight to the front.

Change Step.—The commands are Change Step, MARCH. Being in march at quick time, at the command MARCH, given as the right foot strikes the ground, advance and plant the left foot, plant the toe of the right foot near the heel of the left and step off with the left foot. (Execute the change on the right foot similarly, the command MARCH being given as the left foot strikes the ground.)

To the Rear.—To face to the rear in marching, being in march, the commands are: To The Rear, MARCH. At the command MARCH, given as the right foot strikes the ground, advance and plant the left foot, turn to the right about on the balls of both feet and immediately step off with the left foot.

Other Marchings.—March other than at Attention. The commands are: Route Step, MARCH or At Ease, MARCH. Route Step MARCH, at the command MARCH Volunteers are not required to march at attention or to maintain silence. At Ease, MARCH is the same as Route Step, MARCH, except that Volunteers will maintain silence.

Dismissing the Squad.—The unit being at a halt the leader calls the unit to attention, if they are not at attention, from a point six paces in front of the center of the unit. He then will give the command—DISMISSED. Volunteers are then free to go and do as they please until the next regularly scheduled drill period.

Forming the Platoon.

To form the platoon, which consists of 3 squads—the command, FALL IN will be given by the senior leader facing the area on which he wishes the platoon to form. At this command the unit will form facing the leader with its center 6 paces to his front in 3 parallel lines (each of these lines constitutes a squad). (Should there be insufficient men to form 3 complete squads, skeleton squads of as near equal number as possible will be formed in 3 ranks, squad leaders placing themselves directly behind one another.)

Fig. V.—A Platoon in Column of Squads

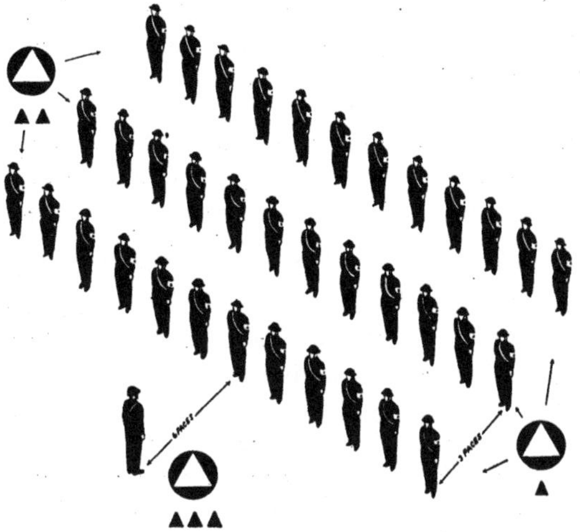

From this formation the unit can march; forward, to the right, or to the left.

Platoon Movements.

At the command: Forward MARCH, each man steps off with his left foot directly to his own front preserving his relative position and so regulates his step that the ranks remain parallel to his original front.

At the command: Right (Left) FACE Forward MARCH, the unit executes a right face on the heel of the right foot and ball of the left foot at the word FACE and at the word MARCH they step off with their left foot as in moving to the front. (Left face is performed by turning on the heel of the left foot and the ball of the right foot.) In the movements to the right or left the commander of the unit takes a position three paces in front of the left file of his command, at double time if necessary.

Being in a column to change direction the commands are—Column Right (Left) MARCH. At the command MARCH, given as the right (left) foot strikes the ground the first man of the leading element on the right (left) advances one step and then steps off in the new direction using half steps until the men to his left (right) are abreast of him. Full step is then resumed.

Close Interval—Normal Interval.—Being in column of threes at normal interval between squads to March or form at Close Interval, the commands are: Close, MARCH. At the command MARCH, the squads close to the center by obliquing until the interval between men is 4 inches. The center squad take up the half step until the dress has been regained.

If this movement is executed from the halt, the squads close toward the center by executing Right or Left Step until 4-inch intervals are reached.

Being in column of threes at close interval between squads to March or form at Normal Interval, the commands are: Extend, MARCH. At the command MARCH, the squads open to the right and left from the center by obliquing until the normal interval is regained.

If this movement is executed from the halt, the squads Right or Left Step until normal interval is regained.

Change Direction.—Being in column of threes to change direction, the commands are: Column Right (Left) MARCH. The right flank man of the leading rank is the pivot. At the command MARCH, given as the right foot strikes the ground, the right flank man of the leading rank faces to the right in marching and takes up the half step until the other men of his rank are abreast of him, then he resumes the full step. The other men of the leading rank oblique to the right in marching without changing interval, place themselves abreast of the pivot man, and conform to his step. The ranks in rear of the leading rank execute the movement on the same ground and in the same manner as the leading rank.

Fig. VI
Forming the Citizens' Defense Corps for Parade

(Services will form and move as platoons)

- ●   Mayor, Defense Coordinator and Dignitaries.
- ☐   Commander, C. D. C.
- ▭   Staff.
- ▭   Messengers.
- ▭   Drivers.
- ☐   Fire Department Chief.
- ▭   Auxiliary Firemen.
- ▭   Rescue Squads.
- ☐   Police Department Chief.
- ▭   Auxiliary Police.
- ▭   Bomb Squads.
- ☐   Colors.
- ☐   Warden Service Chief.
- ▭   Air Raid Wardens.
- ▭   Fire Watchers.
- ▭   Emergency Food Housing Units.
- ☐   Medical Service Chief.
- ▭   Medical Field Units.
- ▭   Nurses' Aides Corps.
- ☐   Public Works Service Chief.
- ▭   Demolition and Clearance Crews.
- ▭   Road Repair Squads.
- ▭   Decontamination Corps.

○

Milton Keynes UK
Ingram Content Group UK Ltd.
UKHW020639180924
1707UKWH00048B/453